ISBN-13: 978-0692212400 (tanya\weinberger)
ISBN-10: 069221240X

tanyaweinberger6911@comcast.net

THE COMPOST PILE

Written and Illustrated by
TANYA WEINBERGER

We all benefit from composting.
It's easy! It's fun! It's so worth doing!
We can all recycle organic matter into the fertilizer
that will feed our planet
so that it can continue to
feed us.
COMPOST!

In this book the creatures who live in the compost pile will guide you easily and delightfully through the valuable art of composting. And after you've read the following pages you can perform *The Compost Rap*, found on the last pages, to your friends.

When you have learned how to create a compost pile, you can create one in your backyard, or contribute your organic waste to your neighbor's pile, or to your community compost pile. The earth will thank you.

For copies of *The Compost Pile* contact: Createspace.com

For information
CONTACT:
Marina A. Bryant, CMP
Author/Artist Representative
770-454-8821
marina.bryant@comcast.net

Dark, crumbly,
earthy smelling,
decomposing organic matter!
This is the
world
of
COMPOST!

Hi boys and girls! I'm Odoriforus, and I'm here to tell you that you can make the earth a better place to live!

Anything that
was once alive
can be composted!

A corner
of your yard
will do.

A wire or wooden enclosure
is efficient
but not necessary.

If you burn wood, you can add the cold ash from your fireplace or wood stove.

ASH

The compost pile teams with bacteria, fungi, protozoans centipedes, beetles and earthworms.

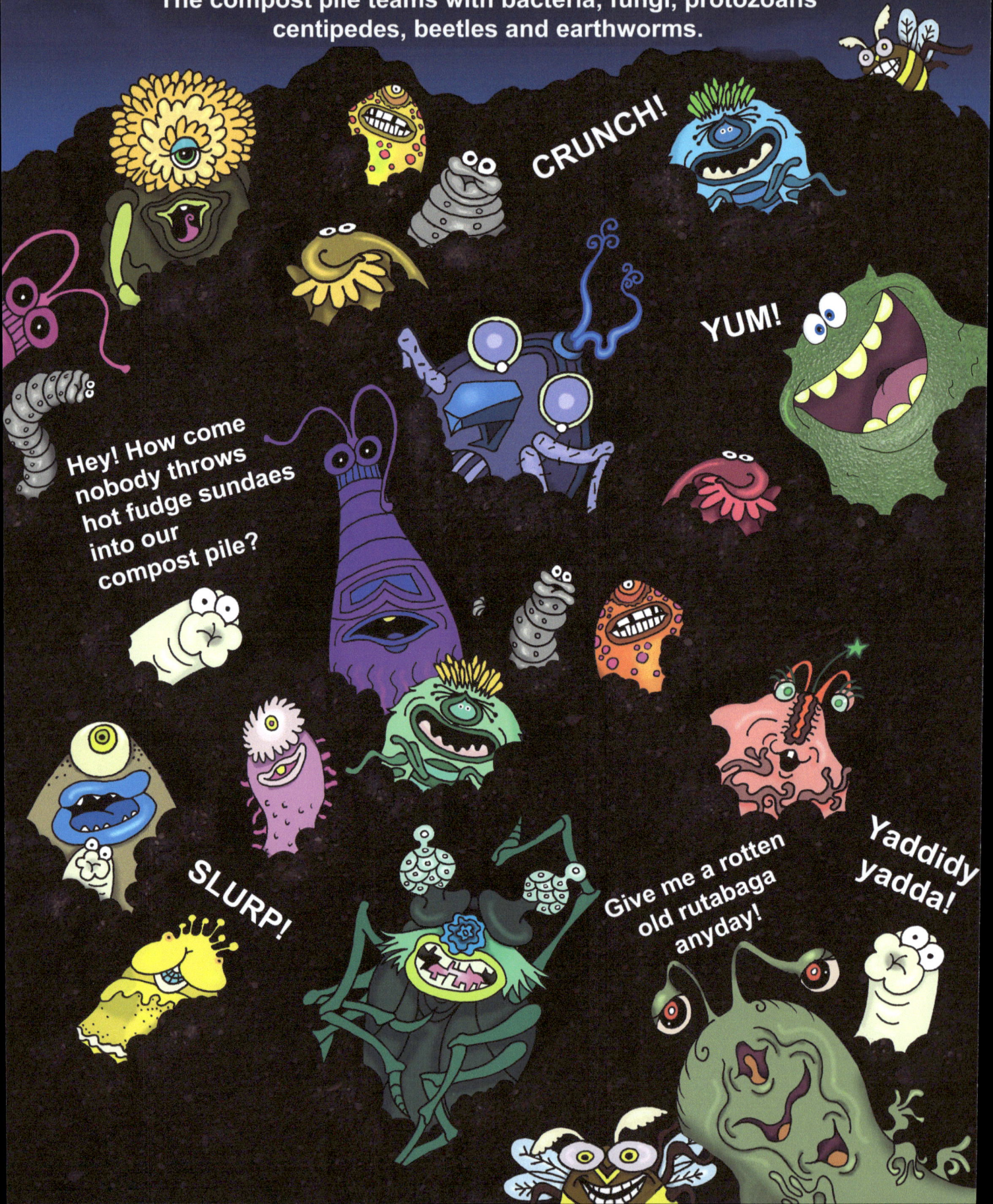

CRUNCH!

YUM!

Hey! How come nobody throws hot fudge sundaes into our compost pile?

SLURP!

Give me a rotten old rutabaga anyday!

Yaddidy yadda!

And this is good!!!
For these little friends break down
this organic matter,
this stuff that was once alive,
into fertilizer
for other
living things.

Thank you!

Yummm!

Thanks!

This compost is fertilizer that is used to make plants and vegetables grow big and healthy.

Really huge!

...Horse, cow, sheep, chicken, duck, and pig poop!
or a bag of dry manure from the store will do.

All living things need air.
So stir up that pile
with a pitchfork or rake to
let in that air.

CRACK!

BOOM!

All living things
need water too.
Rain helps, but sometimes
you have to add water
from the hose.

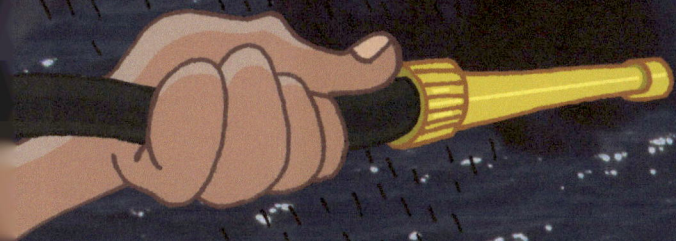

BUZZZZZ

BUZZZ

I know you girls and boys just love to mow that lawn!
So add those lawn clippings to your pile too.
Weeds and dead plants are great too.

BUZZZ

And don't forget those leaves that fall off the trees in the Fall.

And if you don't have a garden
to fertilize with your compost,
I'm sure some of your neighbors
would just love to get
some of that organic matter
for their gardens.

Makes a
great holiday gift!
And don't forget
birthdays. And maybe
your town has a
community compost pile
to which you
can contribute.

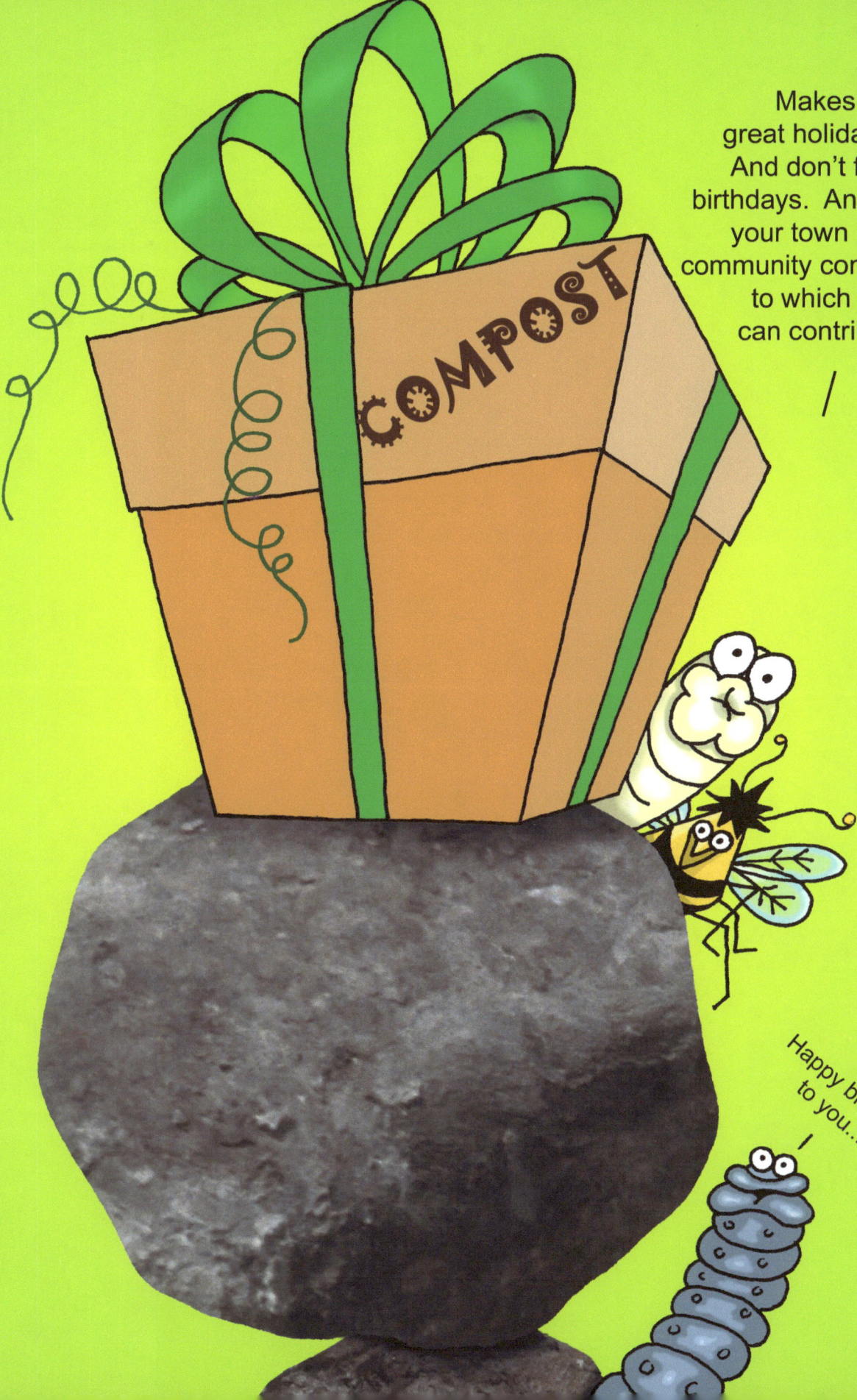

COMPOST

Happy birthday
to you...

If possible,
cut up your organic matter before adding it
to your pile. The smaller the pieces, the faster it
will break down into fertilizer.

This is Odoriforus saying 'Do your share! If it was once alive, COMPOST IT!!!'

The Compost Rap

Pile it up and keep it damp.
Stir it 'round to break it down.
Add some grass and leaves and ash,
garbage, fish heads, bones and trash.
Take your pooper scooper to a local farm.
Get some cow, horse, sheep poop to keep it warm.
Anything that was once alive
will make your compost pile thrive.

Don't waste organic matter
by sending it in a truck
to landfills that don't need
all that glorious mulch and muck.
Digested by the beetles and worms,
fungi, wiggles, munchies, squirms.
And when it's dark with an earthy smell,
it will fertilize your garden well!
It's gotta be hot
if it's gonna rot!

by Tanya Weinberger

Cross off those items
you should *not* put in your compost pile.

buttons   nails   tennis shoes   ash   pickles

pine cones   mushrooms   fish bones   sand   T-shirt

bicycle tire   walnut shells   egg shells   soup

waffles   old socks   computer disks   banana peels

tuna can   pepperoni   piggy bank   potato skins   cheese

coffee grounds   gum wrappers   postage stamps

fish bones   dog food   plastic dinosaurs   broccoli

comic book   paint brush   jewelry   screwdriver

phone book   spoon   cookies   parsley   toothpaste

your homework   onion skins   pencils   chicken feathers

lipstick   soap   gravy   peas   rutabega   watermellon

prunes   cow manure   sawdust   leaves   moldy bread

crayons   photographs   corn flakes   pancakes   caviar   pie

*   *   *

Meats and fats may attract unwanted varments to your compost pile.
So if you must add them, mix them well with ash first and bury them deep in the pile.

Only paper made of natural fibers may be added after being shredded into small pieces.

Never add plastics or chemicals. If you're not sure about an item, don't add it to your compost pile.

TANYA WEINBERGER has led a very lively and interesting life as an award winning animator, writer and producer of short films and videos for televion and international festivals. She has also applied her creative magic to song writing, jewelry designing, sheep farming and fossil hunting.

She now divides her time and creative energies between writing and illustrating books for kids, and wandering the beautiful beaches of Florida hunting for shark teeth, while ideas for future projects fill her ever animated and giggling brain.

Tanya is the published author of two children's books, *GRACE*, and *MS.GRAVITY*, based on her animated short films shown on Nickelodeon HBO, USA, and more.

Her new book, *Grey Matter With a Pinch of Cayenne*, is now available online at Createspace.com.

www.ingramcontent.com/pod-product-compliance
Lightning Source LLC
Chambersburg PA
CBHW041556040426
42447CB00002B/195